THE 7 KEYS TO UNLOCKING THE SECRETS OF YOUR CITY'S BUDGET

2nd Edition

A citizen's guide to watching the public's money

Mary Jo Zenk

Important Disclaimer: This publication is intended to provide general information and should not be construed as legal advice or opinion concerning any specific facts or circumstances. The author does not make any warranties, expressed or implied, with respect to the information in this publication. The author shall not be liable for any incidental or consequential damages in connection with, or arising out of the use of this book.

ISBN-10: 1460915003
ISBN-13: 978-1460915004

DEDICATION

To Chuck, David and Kathryn

ACKNOWLEDGMENTS

The idea for this book grew out of classroom discussions with my graduate students in the government finance course I teach at California State University Monterey Bay. As we looked at many city budget documents, it became clear that some important data was buried under pages of numbers and tables. We wanted understandable budget information to be made available to average citizens concerned about how their government spends money.

Over the years, I have met many people who are actively involved in their communities and deeply concerned about how their city spends taxpayers' money. I have assisted several citizens' groups as they analyzed their cities' budgets and made recommendations to the city councils.

Many have told me how confused they are about their city's budget and how financial decisions are made. They feel there are "secrets" in the document and they want to know how to "unlock" these budget secrets. They have asked for my help and I decided to give it my best.

For the development and production of this book, I am deeply grateful to:

- My husband and children for their support and encouragement during this process.
- My parents, Dave and Germaine Zenk, for their constant love and support.
- To Julie Cavassa who encouraged me and helped me start writing.
- To Nikki Ashley who helped me with the initial design and layout.
- To Chuck Hackett for the many hours of editing and proofing and excellent suggestions.

TABLE OF CONTENTS

The 7 Keys To Unlocking The Secrets of Your City's Budget

INTRODUCTION

Thomas Jefferson believed that self government was not possible unless the citizens were educated sufficiently to enable them to exercise oversight. As concerned citizens, you have the right to know how your local tax dollars are spent. You want to understand why some programs and positions that benefit the community, like after-school activities and additional police officers get cut at the same time the city builds a parking garage or purchases several new vehicles.

The city's[1] budget document provides this information but it is often hard to find and even harder to understand. Most citizens are not accountants and do not have time to take a course in government finance.

---

[1] By city we mean any local municipal government. The local municipal government may also be called a borough, town, township, or village.

If you cannot read the budget, how are you going to know if your money is being put to good use? How are you going to hold your elected officials accountable?

> *Whenever the people are well informed, they can be trusted with their own government; that whenever things get so far wrong as to attract their notice they may be relied on to set them to rights.*
>
> Thomas Jefferson, 1789 to Richard Price, ME 7:253

This 7 Keys book is intended to help you find the most important information in your city's budget document. Whether you are a concerned citizen, a neighbor appointed to serve on a city commission, a volunteer firefighter, a newly elected official, or a student of local government, my hope is that this book will guide you toward a better understanding of the city's budget and help you become more effectively involved in your city's decision-making process.

When it comes to municipal government budgets there is not a 'one size fits all' approach. While there are rules governing financial reporting statements, there is no such requirement for how a city presents its budget information. There are recommended 'best practices' and award programs[2] sponsored by national and state industry associations; and some states require local governments to include specific information in their budget documents.

---

[2] The Government Finance Officers' Association has published a number of best practices for government budgets and offers a Distinguished Budget Presentation Award program.

Yet, at the end of the day, we are left with a variety of binders, books, presentations, reports, web pages, and city council resolutions – all claiming to be the budget document.

Even though the documents may look significantly different, there are several elements in most city finance structures and budgets that are common to all. This guide identifies those common elements in order to help you understand your city's budget.

The format of this book provides basic information about certain key sections of a city's budget and helps you locate that information in your own city's budget document.

As you read the book, you will be asked to find information pertinent to your city's budget. Some of the questions in this book will ask you to find summary information in your city's budget document. The information is fairly common financial information used by most cities.

You might want to have a notebook available to write down this information and where you found it in the budget document.

    ✎ I will use this pencil in hand symbol to identify important items for your notebook. You may also locate some helpful pages in the budget document, print them out and include them in your notebook.

By doing this, you will be creating your own personal reference guide to your city's budget document, which will help you quickly find the information later. Every good investigator or detective has a notebook.

If you have trouble locating this summary information, you may want to ask the city to include it in future budget documents.

With the increase in public attention to government accountability, citizens demand more transparency and are looking for tools or keys to find the most important information among the numerous public documents and pages available to them. This book is written to help average citizens find and understand the key issues in the city's budget.

The city's budget document holds the secrets to the overall financial health of your city government. These seven keys have helped my students unlock those secrets. I hope they will help you, as well.

The budget document shows the major revenue and spending decisions of the local government. It reflects the financial impact of decisions made by local elected officials.

1ST KEY: OPEN THE DOOR
WELCOME TO CITY HALL

The first key to understanding your city's budget is to gather basic information about your city and the services provided.

What is a city?
A municipal government is an incorporated area independent of a county or state government that has its own governing and taxing authority. There are several names for municipal governments in the United States, including: cities, boroughs, towns, townships, and villages. This book focuses on municipal governments and uses "city" to mean any municipal government.

Do you live in a city? Do you live in an unincorporated area of the county[3]?

---

[3] County is the primary governing entity below the state government in 48 states. Connecticut and Rhode Island do not have county governments. The county government is called a borough in Alaska or a parish in Louisiana.

For those who do not live in incorporated municipalities, the county provides these municipal services. Although this book is directed toward city governments, much of it can also be applied to county governments.

Cities are governed by elected officials. There are different names for elected officials such as council members or commissioners. This book will refer to the elected governing body as the "city council".

Even though there are different forms and structures used by municipal governments, they are each required to adopt a budget that provides a plan for how tax dollars are spent for city services.

Basic information about your city

➢ Find the following information and write it in your notebook:
- City name, address, phone number:
- City website:
- Name of mayor or city manager/administrator who is responsible for day-to-day administration:
- Names of the elected officials in your city:
- County name:
- City population: This will allow you to do some comparisons to other cities later. If it is not on your city's website check the U.S. Census website at www.census.gov.

What services does your city provide?

City government responsibilities often include things like public safety, fire and rescue services, maintenance of city streets, parks and recreation, wastewater treatment, trash removal, zoning and building code enforcement, animal control and other essential services. When looking at any city's budget you need to understand what services are included and paid directly by the city. Look on your city's website to see which services your city provides or call city hall and ask the city clerk.

Not all cities provide the same services. It is important to first have some basic information about what services your city provides. Here are some examples of the differences between cities:

- Some have their own police and fire services while others rely on county or regional partnerships to provide one or both of these services.
- A few operate water and/or electric utilities to their residents.
- Some cities collect trash using their own public works department while others contract trash collection to a private firm or another government entity and pay for it with city funds. Some cities choose a private firm to collect the trash and the citizens pay that company directly for their trash collection.
- Some cities manage the local schools and in other communities the school districts are independent of local government.

The table below includes a list of services that cities may provide:

✎ In your notebook, list all the services your city provides.

Identify your city's services

Police	Fire	Emergency response/ambulance
Electricity/Gas	Water	Sewer
Library	Recreation programs	Parks
Community centers	Pools	Golf course
Bus service	Animal control/shelter	Sports programs & fields
Trash	Street maintenance	Sidewalk repair
Schools	School crossing guards	After school activities & youth services
Day care	Senior services	Code enforcement
Airport	Affordable housing	Social services
Building plans & permits	Jail	Hospital/health clinics

What services are provided by other government entities or private firms?

Here are some typical city services that may be provided by another government entity such as the county, another city, or a regional partnership:

- The county government may be responsible for the libraries located in your city.
- A special district may be responsible for providing fire and rescue services.
- Your city may contract with a neighboring city for police services.
- A private company may be contracted by the city government to trim city trees.

These services may be paid directly from your city to the other jurisdiction or paid indirectly through an allocation of local tax dollars. If the city pays another jurisdiction directly for these services, the contract cost will be included in the city's budget. If the services are funded through the allocation of local tax dollars to another jurisdiction, you will not see these services reflected in the city's budget, because the allocation of local tax dollars is generally directed by state and local laws.

Increasingly, more cities are contracting certain services, such as landscaping to private companies. Some cities contract directly for these services and the cost for these contracts are included in the budget. Some city services, such as trash collection, may be awarded to a private firm and the citizens pay fees directly to the private firm for these services. These costs are not included in the city's budget.

This book focuses on the services paid directly by your city government, even if these services are contracted to another government or private firm.

⊱ See if you can figure out which of the services shown on page eight are provided by another government agency or private firm and paid for by your city. In your notebook list the service(s) your city pays another government agency or private firm to provide. These services will be included in the budget document but usually do not have city positions associated with them. This may not be easy to determine. You may need to contact city hall for some help.

1st Key Summary

The first key to understanding your city's budget is gathering basic information about your city and knowing what services are provided and paid for by the city

It is common to want to compare your city to others in the county or the state. However, it is difficult to truly compare cities if they provide different services. It would be the same as comparing apples to oranges.

More and more cities are posting information on their websites about the city and the services provided. Do you know what services your city provides directly? Do you know which services are contracted to other jurisdictions and private firms? Is this information available on the city's website?

Another way to compare services to other cities is to perform a few basic calculations based on the city's population. Some cities have a very small population and provide very limited services and others have a very large population and provide a full range of services. Knowing the size of your city will help you in comparing it to other cities. Later in this book, you will see examples of these types of calculations, such as the cost of library services per resident.

What additional information would you like to see made available on your city's website?

What city services are you particularly interested in knowing about?

> **A glossary of terms is included at the end of this book that are common in many city budget documents, including terms pertaining to other city funds, not just the general fund.**

2ND KEY: OPEN THE BOOK
HOW TO READ THE BUDGET DOCUMENT

The second key to understanding your city's budget is to find the city's budget document and summary information.

Many cities now post their budget document on the city's website. Some have the document available as one downloadable document file. This may be a very large file. Other cities provide a table of contents with a link to each section.

If your city does not have the budget on its website, it should be available for review and/or purchase at the city hall offices. The purchase price generally covers the cost for copying/printing the document. The budget document may also be available for review at the city's main library.

You can contact your city hall office and ask how you can review or purchase the city's budget document.

You should have no problem finding your city's budget document. If you do, check with your state's open records law which is similar to the federal Freedom of Information Act (FOIA) to find out how to access the budget.

There are also 'sunshine laws' in most states that require government meetings, including budget discussions, to be open to the public. The agenda needs to be advertised ahead of time. These sunshine laws have different names in various states.

Let's find your city's budget document

To find your city's budget document first look at your city's website. There may be a link to the budget document on the home page of the website. If not, type in the word "budget" in the search field of the city's website to help you find the budget document. Sometimes it can be found on the finance department's web page.

The budget document itself can be quite lengthy. Do not be discouraged by the size. You do not need to read every page of the document to understand it. This book will identify the key sections of the document that will provide the important budget information you need.

❧ Once you find the web page with the budget documents, look for the most recent adopted or proposed budget document. In your notebook write down the web address so you can find it again quickly.

Depending on what time of year you are looking for the budget and how close it is after the beginning of the city's fiscal year[4], there may only be a proposed or recommended budget document for the current fiscal year. It often takes a few weeks or more after the fiscal year[4] begins for staff to produce the adopted budget document because there is usually a lot of supplementary information included in this document.

When is the beginning of your city's fiscal year?
- January 1st
- April 1st
- July 1st
- October 1st

Budget documents can be very large. Depending on the speed of your computer and internet access, it may be easier to download the budget document onto your computer to find the information asked for in this guide.

---

[4] Fiscal Year – A fiscal year is sometimes called a budget year. It is a period used for calculating the annual financial statements of an organization. Many local governments start their fiscal year on July 1st. The federal government starts its fiscal year on October 1st.

Biennial budgets

Most cities adopt their budget annually. Some cities adopt a budget every two years, called a biennial budget. One of the purposes of a biennial budget is to be more fiscally conservative and consider the longer term impact of decisions on the city's budget. Another reason is to be more cost efficient, since there is a considerable amount of staff time spent preparing a budget.

Since the 2008-2009 recession, some governments with biennial budgets have had to adopt a new budget for the second year in order to reflect a more accurate financial picture.

✎ Look at your city's budget document for the time period covered. Write down in your notebook whether your city's budget is an annual or biennial budget. If your city produces a biennial budget you may need to find an amended budget for the second year.

Let's find summary information about your city's budget

Because the city's budget is often a large and complex document, many cities provide summary information to help explain the budget. This summary information may include both a narrative section and tables and graphs with financial information. Typical summary documents include budget-in-brief, budget presentation, and the budget message.

Budget-in-Brief

Some cities produce a budget summary, sometimes called a 'budget-in-brief' or a 'citizen's guide to the budget.' This is usually a newsletter or brochure format with just a few pages summarizing the much more detailed budget document. Some may also highlight city achievements.

  ✎ Does your city have a budget-in-brief document? If so, write down the web address where you found this budget-in-brief. If you found it helpful, you may want to include a copy of it in your notebook. Can you see how a summary document like this makes the budget information more accessible for most citizens?

If your city does not have a budget-in-brief, you might want to encourage them to prepare one in the future so that more citizens can understand the budget decisions.

Budget Presentation

The city staff presents a recommended budget to the city council for their discussion, deliberation and approval at a public meeting. Sometimes this information is available on the city's website as a PowerPoint presentation. It may be included on the same web page as the budget document or on the city council web page.

Some cities include memoranda, reports and presentations on the web page that has city council agendas. There may also be a staff memorandum to the council that includes the proposed resolution for adopting the budget.

This resolution is the legal authorization for the adoption of the budget. It shows the level of budget authorization provided to the city manager to spend money in accordance with the budget. If any of these authorized categories change, the staff would have to request a budget amendment from the city council.

For example, the council usually adopts a total budget for each fund. If the council also adopts 'line item' budgets for each department within each fund, then any changes to any of these budget line items would require approval by the council during the year

✎ Try to locate any budget presentation or staff memoranda regarding the city's budget. Review this summary information to get an overall picture of the city's budget situation and the major issues facing the city. Does this document help you understand your city's budget? Write down where you found this information in your notebook. If you found this information helpful you might want to print it out for your notebook.

If the information is not on-line, you can ask the city clerk for a copy of the staff report, resolution and any presentation about the budget that was made to the city council at a public meeting.

Budget Message or Transmittal Letter

In the budget document there is usually a budget message, transmittal letter or some other introductory message prepared by the city manager or mayor. This document usually provides a narrative description of the economic situation, major issues facing the city, and any changes in services from the previous year.

✎ There may also be a budget summary narrative included in the budget document, especially if the budget message or transmittal letter is short. Find the budget message, transmittal letter and/or the budget summary in the budget document. Does this document help you understand the city's budget situation? Write down the page numbers of the budget document for this summary information. If you found this document helpful, you might want to make a copy and include it in your notebook.

Mission, Vision, Value Statements and Strategic Goals and Objectives

Just like businesses and nonprofit organizations, some cities have mission, vision or value statements and strategic goals and objectives. These statements are usually prepared separately from the budget process and adopted by the city council after public discussion.

These statements of purpose may be shown on the city's website or in another city document. They can help the governing body prioritize and make annual budget decisions with the long term goals and the vision of the city in mind.

Sometimes the budget message or other narrative sections in the budget document specifically refer to the city's mission, vision and value statements or the strategic goals and objectives in explaining why certain budget decisions were made.

> ✎ Find your city's mission and vision or value statements and any strategic goal statements and objectives. What are they? Do any of the budget summary documents (budget-in-brief, budget presentation, or budget message) refer to these long term vision statements or strategic goals? If you found this information, write down where you found it in your notebook.

Major revenue issues

Revenue means all the money coming into the city, including taxes, fees, and grants. Read the budget message and summary information that you found previously. Search for information about the city's revenue in these same budget summary documents. There may be a separate narrative section in the budget document that discusses each of the city's revenue sources.

    ❘ What are the major revenue issues facing your city? How is the city addressing these issues in this budget? In your notebook, write down where you found any discussion of major revenue issues facing your city.

The fourth key section of this book will describe the typical revenue sources most city governments rely on.

Major expenditure issues

Expenditure simply means the money to be spent by the city. Cities provide services and not products so the bulk of their expenditures for these services are personnel costs or contracts.

    ❘ Read these same budget summary documents and search for information about the city's expenditures and the services provided. In your notebook write down where you found any discussion of major expenditure issues.

There may be a discussion regarding the addition or deletion of staff positions, or changes in personnel costs. These types of changes have a direct impact on services The fifth key section of this book will discuss city expenditures and the sixth key will explain personnel cost information.

❦ What major expenditure issues are facing the city? What services are being changed from last year? In your notebook write down the page numbers of the budget document that describe the major expenditure issues.

2nd Key Summary

The second key to understanding your city's budget is to learn how to find your city's budget document and to review any budget summary information.

Did you find your budget document online or did you have to go to city hall?

Does your city have summary information about the budget? Is it easy to find? Is it understandable? Does the summary information explain the major revenue and expenditure issues facing the city? Does the summary information explain what the numbers mean in a narrative format? Are there helpful graphs, tables?

What would you like to see your city do to make the budget more accessible and understandable for citizens?

Does your city have any long term purpose statements such as a mission, vision or value statements and strategic goals and objectives? Does any of the summary information refer to these statements? Is there a clear link between these long term priorities and the budget decisions that were made?

3RD KEY: TURN THE PAGE
UNDERSTANDING THE GENERAL FUND

The third key to understanding the city budget is to learn about the general fund.   Funds are used by governments to separate and account for certain revenue and expenditures for specific reasons.   A very simple way to understand these government funds is to think of them as separate household bank accounts. You may have a general checking account, several savings accounts, an investment account, accounts for your children's college funds, and your retirement accounts.

Just as there are some legal restrictions on certain accounts, such as your retirement and children's college funds, most government funds have restrictions. Using funds help governments account and report how they spend designated revenue for specific purposes.

All cities have a general fund which is where they account for most of their basic services, such as police, fire, public works, and city council. There are no external restrictions on how the city spends its money in the general fund. Learning about the general fund budget will give you a very good understanding of the city's fiscal situation and what decisions the city council adopted to provide a balanced budget.

Cities may have several restricted funds. These funds have some legal limitations on how the revenues can be used. For example, your city may collect a certain fee that can only be used for a specific purpose, such as a sewer line in a neighborhood. Another example is a parcel tax, approved by the voters, for a specific purpose such as the library. These designated fees or tax revenues have to be accounted for separately from the general fund.

Cities will often separate their longer term capital projects[5] into one or more funds so that the costs associated with each long term project over many years can be budgeted and accounted for separately.

This book focuses only on the general fund in your city budget. These funds are not restricted. There is more flexibility in how the city chooses to spend this money.

---

[5] Capital projects are physical improvements like parking garages, new city hall, new police cars or major renovations to city buildings.

Some budget decisions, such as salary schedules and benefits, will impact all city funds but it is important to note that any budget savings from these decisions that may impact a restricted fund cannot be used by the general fund.

What is your city's total budget?

Look for a section of the budget document that shows the total budget in your city. This information may also be included in the budget message or transmittal letter. There may be a chart or table that has a column for each of the city's funds. Another place to look for the total budget information is the city council's resolution that may be included in the budget document. If it is not in the budget document, the resolution will be at city hall with other council resolutions.

> ✎ See if you can find the total budget and how much of that total is identified as the general fund. In your notebook write down the amount of the total budget and where you found it so you can find it again.

On the next page there is an example of a pie chart that illustrates a total city budget and the amount of the budget that is the general fund. This percentage will vary for each city depending on the restricted and other funds.

Does your city have a chart like this?

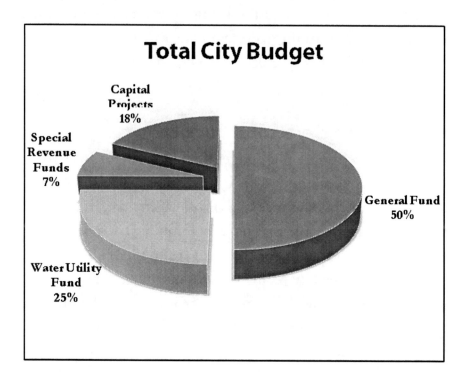

What is the amount of the general fund budget?

Look for summary information about the general fund budget. Often the amount of the general fund budget is specifically mentioned in the budget message or summary narratives. There may be one or more tables that have information specific to the general fund.

✎ Find the answers to the following questions and write them in your notebook along with the page number(s) of the budget document where you found them.

- How much is budgeted for total revenue in the general fund?
- How much is budgeted for total expenditures in the general fund?

What other city funds are included in the budget document?

Other funds that you may find in the budget document include:

- Special revenue funds are restricted for a specific purpose such as an assessment for sewers in a specific neighborhood.
- Enterprise funds, such as a water utility operation.
- Capital project funds for major infrastructure improvements.

✎ In your notebook list three other major funds in the city budget other than the general fund. Can you tell what specific purposes each of these funds serve?

Use of reserves to balance the general fund budget

If the general fund expenditures exceed revenues, the city may need to use reserves to balance the budget. Cities may use other terms for reserves, such as fund balance[6] or rainy day fund. They all refer to the money that has been saved or reserved from prior years. Sometimes these reserves are shown as a revenue source so that the budget presented is shown as balanced.

Can you tell whether your city needed to use any reserves to balance the budget? Does any of the budget summary and narrative discuss the use of reserves to balance the budget?

If the budget summary information is not clear on this topic, look for financial summary information, usually in a table format, that shows the beginning of the year balance in the general fund and the end of the year projected balance.

    ☙ Did your city use reserves to balance the budget? How much? In your notebook write down how much reserves were needed, if any, to balance this budget, and where you found this information.

---

[6] Fund balance is used in government accounting. It is the difference between assets and liabilities.

Does your city have sufficient reserves in the general fund?

Having sufficient available cash is important for any organization, whether a business or nonprofit corporation or a government agency. Many organizations strive to have two to three months of available cash to pay bills.

Most local governments obtain the bulk of their revenues from property taxes that are collected once or twice during the year, so they need to have sufficient cash to cover the monthly costs until those tax revenues are received. If they don't have sufficient cash reserves, they have to borrow funds on a short term basis. The more they borrow the more interest they have to pay each year on this debt.

Many cities have a financial policy that states how much they want to maintain in reserves. Some include these financial policies in their budget document. The Government Finance Officers Association recommends that "general-purpose governments, regardless of size, maintain a balance in their general fund of no less than two months of regular general fund operating revenues or regular general fund operating expenditures."[7]

---

[7] Government Finance Officers Association Best Practice *Replenishing Fund Balance in the General Fund (2011)* available at http://www.gfoa.org.

In recent years, many governments have faced significant reductions in revenues due to the recession and have used cash reserves to balance their budgets. As they restore these reserves, some have revisited their reserve policy and increased the amount of reserves on hand.

⬧ Can you find your city's policy for reserves? Is your city budgeting to restore reserves? How much general fund reserves, fund balances or 'rainy day' strategic reserves does your city have? In your notebook write down how much is the general fund balance they have at the beginning and end of the fiscal year. Do they have at least two months worth of general fund expenditures? Do you think they have sufficient cash reserves?

Example of calculating reserve level

If the total general fund expenditure budget is $75 million
Then two months general fund expenditures is $12.5 million

Now compare the two months of general fund expenditures to the amount of general fund reserves at the beginning or end of the fiscal year.

Does the city have at least $12.5 million in reserves?

3rd Key Summary

Knowing the difference between city funds and focusing on the general fund is the third key to understanding your city's budget.

Other city funds have restrictions on how funds are spent and the city council has little discretion on how these funds are spent. Understanding what activities are included in the various city funds explains why certain types of purchases are made at the same time the city has to reduce other services.

For example, the city may be constructing a new parking garage paid out of a restricted fund designated for that garage at the same time they have to reduce hours at the recreation centers which are in the general fund. Although the timing of this large capital expenditure may seem odd given the cuts in city services - it is coincidental. The decisions were made independent of each other based on specific funding sources requirements.

Because of the restrictions on these other funds, the city council cannot generally move money between these funds unless specifically allowed. They are very limited in how they can spend these restricted funds. That is why city councils spend less time discussing the budget of these other funds, even if they are very large budgets.

Most of the time spent on the city's budget is focused on the general fund?   Do you understand the difference between a city's total budget and general fund budget?

Did your city need to use reserves to balance the budget this year?   Does your city have at least two months of general fund expenditures in reserve?

4TH KEY: FIND THE MONEY
WHERE DOES THE MONEY COME FROM?

The fourth key to understanding the city budget is to learn about the revenues in the general fund. Revenue in the general fund comes from a number of sources. The revenue in the general fund is considered unrestricted so the city can choose how they wish to spend those funds to provide services.

The typical revenue sources of a municipal government's general fund are: property tax, sales tax, hotel occupancy tax (also known as transit occupancy tax or TOT), business license fees, building permits, developer fees, and parking tickets. A few, usually large cities, also have income taxes.

Your city's taxing authority varies depending on what state you live in.

    ✍ Find a table in the budget document that shows the different revenue sources for the general fund. In your notebook write down the page number(s) where you found this information. You might also want to print out this table of general fund revenue. You will be using this table for the following pages.

If the information is not available in the budget document, you might want to ask the finance department for a list of the major revenues in the general fund, with the budget for each.

Major revenue

There may be a large number of revenue sources shown in this table. Hopefully, they are grouped into several large categories, such as property taxes, sales taxes, and fees.

Some budget documents include pie charts or graphs to help visually show the major revenue sources in the general fund, such as the example on the next page.

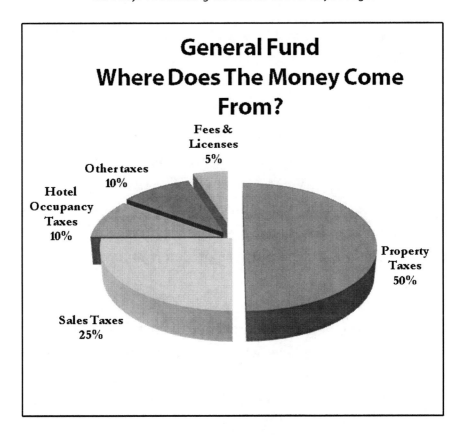

Does your city have a pie chart like the one on this page? If not, look at the table with all revenue sources of the general fund. Typical sources of general fund revenues:

- Property taxes
- Sales taxes
- Hotel Occupancy taxes
- Fees and licenses

  ✎ In your notebook, write down your city's major revenue sources for the general fund.

Let's look at the major revenue sources most cities rely on in their general fund.

Property tax

Many cities have the power to determine their local property tax rate. This property tax rate is multiplied by the assessed value of the property. The assessed value of the property is not the market value of the property. It is the property value determined by a designated government official, often an elected position, for the purpose of determining property taxes.

For most cities, property tax revenue is the primary source of income. Property taxes are also a major source of revenue for other local government agencies, such as school districts. The total property tax bill that the property owner pays may be distributed to several government entities.

How much of your property tax goes to the city?

If you own property you probably pay property tax. If you rent your home, you don't pay property taxes directly. A portion of your rent is used by the property owner to pay property taxes.

> ✎ Take a look at your last property tax bill. Does your tax bill identify how much of your property tax (the percentage or the tax rate) goes to your city? If so, write down the property tax rate or portion of the bill that goes to the city in your notebook.

In some states, counties or cities, the property tax rate is capped by law. In many of these cases, the law to limit the tax rate was passed by the voters so any changes would require another vote. Is your property tax rate capped?

> ✒ Look at the table that shows the revenue sources in the general fund. There may be many individual revenue accounts or line items with similar account names related to property taxes. Look for a summary category for these property taxes. In your notebook answer the following questions:
> - What has the city budgeted for property tax revenue?
> - What portion of the total general fund revenue comes from property tax?

Sales tax

Some cities receive sales tax revenue. Whether a city gets sales tax depends on the state law. Different states have different rules regarding sales tax. Sales taxes are usually collected at the county or state level and distributed to cities and other government jurisdictions based on the laws. Some states allow cities to add a local tax onto the state sales tax. That is why in some states, the sales tax rate differs from city to city. The sales tax rate that you pay as a consumer is distributed to various government agencies.

✍ Look at the table that shows the revenue sources in the general fund. There may be many individual revenue accounts or line items with similar account names related to sales taxes Look for a summary category for these sales taxes.   In your notebook answer the following questions.

- What, if any, has the city budgeted for sales tax revenue?
- What portion of the total general fund revenue comes from sales tax?

What portion of your sales tax dollars, if any, goes to your city?

Some cities are allowed to add a few cents to the state sales tax. For example, the total sales tax rate you pay in local stores is 8/0%. Of that amount, the city gets 2.0%.

✍ See if you can find what portion of the sales tax you pay at the stores located in your city goes to your city and put this in your notebook.   If you cannot find it, ask the city finance staff.

Hotel occupancy tax or transit occupancy tax (TOT)

Another source of revenue for many local governments is the tax charged to people visiting the city, especially hotel guests. Many residents would prefer taxes on visitors be increased rather than property and sales taxes which impact local residents. However, in setting tax rates, cities need to consider what other cities charge for hotel occupancy taxes so that they do not drive away tourists due to exceptionally high rates.

> ✎ Look at the table that shows the revenue sources in the general fund. In your notebook answer the following questions:
>
> - What has the city budgeted for hotel occupancy or transit occupancy tax?
> - What portion of the total general fund revenue comes from hotel occupancy or transit occupancy tax?

<u>What impact does tourism have on your city's budget?</u>

Tourism may be an important source of revenue for your city. Does your city have a large number of hotels/motels? Increasing tourism helps both the city's revenues and local businesses. Your city may be spending some funds to promote tourism in your city as a way to increase both business and government revenue.

If you are interested in learning more about this tax rate, ask the finance department what your city's hotel tax rate is and how it compares to nearby cities.

Other taxes – utility taxes

Your city may collect other taxes, such as a tax on fuel and utilities. These taxes may appear on your utility bills. These taxes generally pay toward the cost of maintaining the city's infrastructure, such as roads, utility poles, and street lights that help deliver these utilities to residents.

    ✎ Look at the table of general fund revenues. In your notebook answer the following questions:
- What, if any, has the city budgeted for revenue from utility taxes?
- What portion of the total general fund revenue comes from utility tax?

Other taxes - Income tax

Not many cities rely on income taxes as a revenue source. Some larger cities that have a significant number of people commuting from the suburbs for work may charge an income tax on those who work in the city to help pay for the city services they use while at work.

    ✎ Look at the table of general fund revenues. In your notebook answer the following:
- Does your city get any income tax revenue?
- If so, how much do they get in income taxes?

How much city income tax do you pay?

If you pay city income taxes, they will be reported on your W2 form, which is used for your federal and state income tax returns.

Take a look at your last W2 form to find out how much, if any, of your income tax dollars went to your city.

Fees, licenses and permits

In addition to taxes, cities collect revenue from fees, licenses and permits. Examples of these include: business licenses, user fees for city owned golf courses and pools, and permit fees for certain construction projects. Some cities charge fees to cover their costs for operating pools or other city facilities. Other cities have chosen to subsidize some portion of the costs so that more residents can participate. Cities may also set permit fees at a similar rate to other cities even if it is less than it costs to deliver services. This encourages new construction and economic development.

☞ Look at the table of general fund revenues. In your notebook answer the following questions:

- What has the city budgeted for fees, licenses and permits?
- What portion of the total general fund revenue comes from fees, licenses and permits?

A word of caution about grant revenues

Be aware of one-time grants with restrictions. These federal or state grants do not appear in the general fund but may require a local commitment of general fund revenue in the future. For example, a federal grant that pays for five additional police officers for three years may require the city to commit to keeping those additional police officers for several years beyond the grant period. After the grant period ended these additional police officers would be included in the city's general fund budget and paid with local tax revenues.

4th Key Summary

The fourth key to understanding your city's budget is to learn where the money comes from for the general fund budget. After completing this section you should have a good idea of the major unrestricted revenue sources for your city.

Go back to the table summary for general fund revenue and find the major revenue sources. Some cities list a number of different revenue accounts that make up property taxes or sales taxes. Were you able to figure out the major categories of revenue sources? What are the top three revenue categories for your city's general fund? What is each category's percentage of the general fund revenue ?

Go back to the budget message or summary to see what it said about these primary revenue sources. What follow-up questions do you have about the city's major revenue sources?

5TH KEY: FOLLOW THE MONEY
WHERE DOES THE MONEY GO?

The fifth key to understanding the city budget is to learn about the expenditures in the general fund – where does the money go? This is where the major budget decisions are made for most city services.

Let's look at the major services that are provided from the general fund. How the city chooses to spend this money reflects the priorities for these services. Governments refer to these costs as expenditures. They can be shown at the department level, such as police, fire, or public works, and also by type of expenditures, such as personnel and operating. Some budget documents include specific budgets by account name, such as salaries, fringe benefits, training, travel, and supplies.

Look through your city's budget document. What level of budget detail of expenditures does your city include in the document?

The budget for your city's services

Go back to the first key and find the list of services that your city provides. You can use that list as you answer questions in this section. Some budget documents include pie charts or graphs to help visually show the general fund expenditures.

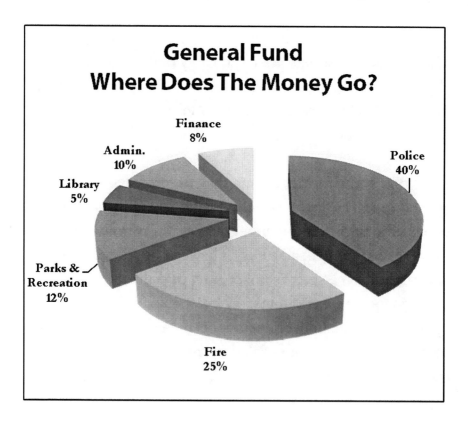

Does your city have a pie chart like this?

☙ Find a table in the budget document that shows the expenditures by each department in the general fund. This information may be in the same summary table as the general fund revenues data. In your notebook write down where you found this information. You might also want to print out this table. You will be using this table for the following pages.

If your city does not have summary information about general fund expenditures at the department level, you may be able to create your own summary table by going to each department's section in the budget and find the total general fund expenditures budgeted. You may want to call the finance department of the city and ask them for this information.

Expenditures by department

Look at the summary table of general fund expenditures by department.

☙ In your notebook create a chart like the one on the next page and list the city departments with the five largest budgets. Which of these has the largest general fund budget? For most cities this will usually be police and/or fire. The city might refer to it as public safety. Divide each department's budget by the total general fund budget to determine what percentage of the city's general fund goes to that department budget.

Top five departments budgeted in the general fund

	Department	$ General Fund Budget	% of General Fund
1.			
2.			
3.			
4.			
5.			
	TOTAL		

Go back to the Budget Message or Transmittal Letter. What does it say about these priority services? Have there been any major changes in service levels since last year? What are they?

Analyzing costs of city services

Once you have the department costs you may want to evaluate these costs in several ways.

- Look at several years and see the rate of increase for a particular department or for the total general fund over time. Compare that with the trend in revenue growth.

- Compare the cost of your city's services with other cities.

Here's an example of comparing two cities general fund budgets. These cities provide the same type of services. The budget for City B has more general fund revenue, a larger population and spends more per person than City A.

	City A	City B
General Fund budget	$68.0 million	$85.0 million
Population	106,000	115,000
General Fund per person	$642 per person	$739 per person

I offer a word of caution when comparing cities. Because of differences between cities, I recommend that you look at several cities with similar size populations to see if your city's per person budget is similar to the norm or significantly different. Also remember that cities provide different services which may explain the cost variance. If there is a significant difference in costs between cities, you will want to investigate further before reaching any final conclusions.

5th Key Summary

The fifth key to understanding your city's budget is to look at the general fund expenditures at the department level. I hope you now have some experience in finding information about specific services and how much they cost. This should give you a good idea of how the city spends its money and what are their priorities. You are learning how to find information in your city's budget document.

Go back to the budget message or summary. Are there any explanations for changes in expenditures or services? For example, the reason for adding two part time recreation activities positions is because of the city's plans (i.e., priority) to provide more sports and afterschool activities to keep children out of trouble or to staff a new community center.

Some budget documents provide more information at the department level, describing the goals, objectives and performance measures. Find the budget for those departments that pique your interest. Many budget documents include detailed information for each department.

This section also provided you with some tools to help you analyze the staffing levels and cost of city services.

6TH KEY: COUNT THE MONEY
PERSONNEL COSTS

The sixth key to understanding the city budget is to learn about the city's personnel costs. The largest expenditure in the general fund for cities is almost always salaries and benefits. This is to be expected since the city's primary purpose is providing service and payroll is the cost of providing those city services.

Public employee salaries and benefits

Historically, many government agencies have provided a better benefit program and less in salaries when compared to the private sector. When public employers had problems recruiting qualified employees, some governments began to increase public sector salaries to be more competitive in the local hiring market.

Most government benefit packages include health insurance and a pension plan. Some benefit packages also include a commitment to pay a portion of the retiree's health insurance. This is called a post retirement benefit.

Public pension plans are similar to the pension plans that many large private sector companies previously offered. These pension plans are called *defined benefit* because the retiree is guaranteed a certain income stream after retirement. Most private sector employers that offer retirement plans have switched to a *defined contribution* plan. These plans, such as 401k, guarantee that a certain contribution to the employee's retirement account will be made by the employer. There is no guarantee as to what the benefits will be upon retirement.

One of the advantages of a defined benefit retirement program is that it helps employers retain employees. Local governments compete with each other for employees, especially for trained positions, such as police. The upfront costs to train some employees, such as police and fire, is significant so governments do not want to lose their trained staff to another jurisdiction offering a better salary and benefit package.

Current issues facing public employers

When the recession hit, many employers in the private sector laid off employees, cut salaries and reduced benefits fairly quickly. It is not as easy to reduce staffing levels, pay and benefits in the public sector for several reasons. The private sector generally responds to decreased demand for products and services when the economy slows by reducing labor costs.

Many positions in the public sector, especially police and fire, require a significant investment and time in training. It takes a long time to hire and train a qualified police officer. Replacing these positions when the economy improves would take considerable time and money so public employers are reluctant to lay off existing trained personnel. Often they choose to not 'fill' vacant positions if they need to reduce labor costs.

In the public sector, the demand for some city services increases when the economy suffers. For example, during the recession there may be more job seekers who use the libraries for internet access to complete online job applications. The demand for access to library services may be increasing at the same time revenue reductions require decisions on where to cut city services.

Another reason public employers appear slower to reduce labor costs during a recession is that most public sector employees are represented by labor unions or collective bargaining units and they have negotiated long term contracts with governments regarding pay, benefits, and also how to handle layoffs. Changes to these terms have to be renegotiated and that process can take time.

The types of common labor cost reductions that local governments negotiate with unions include:

- Salary reductions, either across the board reductions in pay or reducing hours through furloughs.
- Increasing the portion of health insurance costs paid by the employee.
- Changing health insurance plans to a lower cost plan.
- Reducing benefit packages for new hires. Many of the retirement plans for new hires are less generous than the current plans.
- Creating early retirement incentives and 'buy out' programs to encourage existing employees, especially those able to take retirement to do so. This creates vacant positions that they can 'freeze' and not rehire until the economy improves.

Commonly used definitions when discussing personnel costs

Here are some common terms used in city governments when discussing personnel and payroll costs.

Cost of Living Allowance or COLA: This is the automatic annual rate increase for salaries. It is usually negotiated in collective bargaining agreements.

Full Time Equivalent or FTE: Because some positions are part time, governments convert the part time positions to an equivalent full time position. For example, a full time worker works 40 hours a week and a part time worker who works 20 hours a week is calculated as .5 FTE. Or a part time worker who works 15 hours a week is calculated as .375 FTE.

> **Don't be confused by decimals, such as 1.25 FTEs. This means there are part time workers included in the position count.**

Furloughs: Temporary, mandatory, unpaid days off, usually spread out over the year or during a slow period. For example, the city may furlough staff one day per week and close its offices to the public every Friday to save money.

Let's look at your city's budget for total number of positions

- ✒ Find a city-wide organizational chart in the budget document. In your notebook, make a note of the page numbers in the budget document where you found this chart. You might want to make a copy of it for your notebook.

- ✒ Also, find the summary section of workforce or positions. This may be on a separate chart with comparisons from the prior year[8]. The number of city employees or full time equivalent positions may be mentioned in the budget message. Or it may be included in the organizational chart. In your notebook write down the number of city employees or full time equivalents that are in this year's budget. What was the change from the previous year?

If the city does not have this information summarized in the budget document you may be able to create your own summary table by going to each department's section in the budget and find the total FTEs or positions budgeted. You can also call the finance department of the city and ask them for this information

---

[8] Many tables compare current budget year information with at least the prior year's budget information. Some tables will include more than two years of information for comparison.

Go back to the budget message or transmittal letter and look at what it says about the number of positions. Does it explain why there was an increase or decrease in the number of positions? How many, and from which departments? Does it explain how that will impact service levels? Will the city be contracting out any of these services? How does this compare to the city's mission and strategic goals?

Comparing staffing levels in cities

One way to help you evaluate how efficient your city is in providing services is by comparing staffing levels with other cities offering similar services. A simple calculation can be done by dividing the number of positions doing a particular service by the total population. The problem with that is it makes it difficult to compare different size cities. Another way to calculate staffing levels and comparing across cities is to compare the number of positions per 1,000 residents.

Example of calculation:

The number of sworn police positions is 402

The city's population of 123,592 divided by 1,000 is 123.59

Divide these two to get:

The number of sworn police positions per 1,000 residents = 3.25

You can compare staffing levels across cities for different departments this way or for the entire staff funded by the general fund.

Again, I remind you that there are significant differences between cities, so do not rely on this calculation as the sole evaluation tool. It can only give you an indication of your city's staffing level compared to others.

If your city's budget includes non-general fund budgets, such as a water utility or special revenue funds, the total number of positions would include the staffing for these non-general fund activities.

> ✎ Try to find the number of positions that are included in the general fund budget and include that in your notebook. Is that number significantly different from the number of positions in the total budget? Did that number change from the previous year?

Let's look at your city's costs for salaries

Go back to the budget message or transmittal letter and look at what it says about salaries.

Was there a cost of living adjustment (COLA) mentioned? Will the city be reducing labor costs by a furlough or reduction in salaries and by how much? Were there different rates for different bargaining units? If this information is not included in the budget message, check with the city clerk or human resources office for any public document pertaining to negotiated COLAs, salary increases, decreases, and furloughs.

   ■ Is there a salary schedule for all positions included in the budget document? In your notebook write down where you found the salary schedule. It might be located on the city's website under human resources.

Let's look at your city's costs for benefits

Go back to the budget message or transmittal letter and look at what it says about benefits for employees. What does the message say about health care insurance costs paid by the city? What portion of health care costs, if any, are employees paying?

What does the message say about retirement costs? Does the city have to make larger contributions to the pension plan? Most pension plans rely not only on annual contributions but also on certain assumptions regarding income from investments to have sufficient funds to pay out retirement benefits. If these investment assumptions do not materialize, the amount of annual contributions has to increase in order to ensure there are sufficient funds to pay out the defined retirement benefits.

Not all cities include this type of information in their budget documents unless it has become a significant budget issue. Many cities work with a number of unions and have different agreements pertaining to pay and wages so this information may not be in the budget document. You may want to ask the human resources office for a summary of the salary and benefit information across all city employee unions.

Let's look at your city's unfunded retirement liabilities

Retirement obligations have become a huge concern for many local governments. This means they do not have enough funds in the retirement account along with investment projections to meet the promises they made to employees regarding their retirement. With a defined benefit package they have committed to paying their retirees a certain amount each year. Some cities have significant unfunded retirement liabilities.

Does the budget message refer to any retirement obligations the city has to cover? What does it say?

Another issue that has become a concern for some cities is the cost for post retirement benefits. These cities agreed to pay all or a portion of health insurance for their retirees for some period of time. Many of them did not put funds aside for this obligation. They paid this bill annually. Because of the escalating costs of health insurance, this post retirement obligation is now costing them a sizeable portion of their budget.

If you are interested in learning more about your city's unfunded liability obligations, the city's most recent audited financial statements may include some information about this in the Notes section.

Let's look at your city's compensation packages for elected officials and senior management positions

Another emerging concern is the compensation package of elected officials and senior management. People want to know if what they pay their elected officials and city administrators is reasonable.

There is significant media attention when a particular city is found to be paying their elected officials or senior management some combination of salary, stipends, health benefits, retirement, housing, vehicle, and/or travel that is substantially higher than other local governments.

The costs for the compensation packages of elected officials and senior management are included in the adopted budget but are usually presented as a sum for all the positions in one or more city department(s) budgets. The authorization for these payments may be based on the city's charter or adopted by the city council in a separate meeting.

A quick way to calculate the compensation for the city council is to divide the total personnel budget for the city council department by the number of council members. It should be noted that the personnel costs may also include the city clerk and other administrative support so this may not be an accurate calculation. The information on what elected officials make should be public information so you could ask the city clerk for it.

Some cities provide this information on their website. Several states publish this information for all jurisdictions.

> ◈ Look in the budget document, city or state website to see if you can find the costs paid to your city council members. Write down this information in your notebook. If it's not there you may ask the city clerk. Does the budget for what is paid to council members seem reasonable? How much time do they spend on the city's business? Are they full or part time?

Compensation for the city manager

The city manager's salary and benefit package should be a matter of public record. The city manager is one of the few positions directly hired by the city council and the compensation package would be approved in a public meeting. You can contact the city clerk for a copy of the resolution approving the compensation package for the city manager.

The city manager's salary may be listed on the city's salary schedule. Some states are encouraging or requiring cities to post this information on their websites and some states are posting this information on their website for all jurisdictions.

≥ Look in the budget, city or state websites to find compensation package for the city manager. If it's not there you may ask the city clerk. Write this down in your notebook. Does the amount budgeted for salary, and benefits for the city manager seem reasonable compared to other cities?

6th Key Summary

The sixth key to understanding your city's budget is to learn about the costs for government employees. Personnel costs are almost always the single largest expense for local governments. Understanding how your city budgets salary and benefit costs will help you participate in the budget process. Did you find the answer to the following questions?

- How many positions or FTEs are included in the city budget this year? Was there a change from the previous year?
- How many of these positions or FTEs are included in the general fund budget?
- What, if any, changes have been made to salaries and benefits?
- Does the city have any liability for unfunded retirement contributions or post retirement benefits?
- What are the issues related to salary and benefits that are identified in the budget? How is the city addressing them in this budget?
- What questions do you still have about personnel costs that you could not find in the budget document?

7TH KEY: WATCH THE MONEY
GET INVOLVED

The seventh and final key to understanding the city budget is finding out how to get involved in your city's budget process. After using the other six keys to learn about your city's budget, you now have the basic knowledge of your city's budget and the terminology to effectively engage in budget deliberations. These budget sessions are open to the public.

It is best to get involved in the budget process as early as possible. Preparing the budget is a very detailed process and takes a long time. Any significant changes to the budget are best discussed early on so the city staff has the time to cost them out and determine the impact to the entire city budget. Certain decisions in one department may have a ripple effect throughout the city.

It takes time for staff to analyze the budget impact of certain ideas. Some suggestions are simple and impact only one department or one fund. Other ideas may impact multiple departments or require a different staffing structure in the city. Some good budget decisions may not be implemented until later in the fiscal year. They first require policy or procedural changes that need to be written and approved prior to implementing them.

Know when to get involved

> You need to know when your city council discusses budget issues. In the budget document look for a section that describes the budget calendar or schedule. In your notebook write down the page number(s) in the budget document where you found the budget schedule or print it out. This information may also be listed separately on the city council's website.

Earlier in this book you were asked to determine when your city's fiscal year began. When does your city's fiscal year begin? Many city councils start discussing budget priorities about 6-9 months before the fiscal year begins. When does your city council first begin discussing next year's budget in public meetings? If it's not in the budget document, call the finance department or city clerk and ask when the council will have initial budget strategy sessions for the upcoming year.

I recommend that you attend these initial budget or strategy sessions where the council learns about the financial issues facing the city in the coming year and hopefully begins to discuss priorities. If the city has a long term vision and mission statement and strategic goals, this would be a good time to review them and consider how the city may be able to work towards them in the next budget year. Sometimes, because of the economic situation the city faces, it is clear that some of these long term goals may need to be put 'on hold' until the city's financial situation improves.

This is also a good time for the city council to get input from the community to help them prioritize city services. Cities should try to get this input from as many residents as possible, not just from those that show up to city council meetings.

The city staff will take a few months to prepare a recommended budget and bring it back to the council for discussion and adoption. Some city councils will discuss their budget over several months and others over a few weeks.

This is an important time to participate in these budget meetings and help your city council make good budget decisions.

7th Key Summary

The seventh key to understanding your city budget is to know when and how to get involved in the process. You need to know when to get involved in the budget process to have an impact on the budget decisions.

Find the city's budget calendar or schedule to know when the city council will be discussing the budget.

Bring any suggestions about the budget to the city early in the budget process. They will need enough time to study and work through the implementation of any substantive changes.

This is a good time to keep the city's mission, vision, or value statements and strategic goals and objectives in front of the city council. These statements can be used to help the city prioritize budget decisions.

CONCLUSION

The city's budget document is one of the most visible and tangible signs pointing to the overall financial health of your local government.   However, as you have seen, the budget is often a very lengthy document and difficult for most citizens to understand.   This book has hopefully provided you with some basic information necessary to understand the general fund portion of the city's budget. The general fund is where the city council has the most discretion on budget decisions.

I have recommended that you keep a notebook handy as you read this book and review your city's budget document. Throughout these pages, I have suggested things to print out or write down in your notebook along with the page number where you found it.   If you do this, you will have your own personal reference guide to your city's budget that you can quickly refer to months later.   You can also use it to help you find the important information in future budget documents.

You have hopefully learned about your city's general fund revenues, including the various taxes and fees that your city collects and the impact of the local economy on these revenues. You may now begin to understand how the local economic situation might impact government revenue and how local revenue is distributed among various city services, from public safety to parks and recreation. This should help you evaluate the choices the city has to make regarding spending priorities and services. It will also help you consider revenue sources for the city and how to increase revenue to pay for additional services.

Whether you visited city hall or found the city's website, you have, by now, certainly realized that the journey toward a final budget document takes months. The calendar of scheduled public meetings, hearings, and work sessions on the budget can be daunting.

By using this 7 Keys book to help you review your city's budget document you will most likely have some follow-up questions for your city either for the city council or the staff. If you were not able to find some of this summary information, you might ask your city to include this type of information in future budget documents.

I believe these keys will help most citizens understand their city's budget and any significant budget issues. I've summarized the seven keys with the following questions:

(1) What services does your city provide? What do they contract out and to whom? How large is your city?

(2) What are the major budget issues facing your city? What are your city's mission, vision, and strategic goals?

(3) What is your city's total budget? What is your city's general fund budget? Does the city have any general fund reserves?

(4) General fund budget – Where does the money come from? What are the major revenue sources for your city's general fund? What are the major issues that may impact these revenues?

(5) General fund budget – Where does the money go? What services or departments have the largest budget? What service levels are different from last year and how will they impact residents? Why?

(6) Personnel costs – What is the total number of FTEs in the city? How has that changed from the prior year? Why? What are the changes to salaries and benefits from the prior year? Does the city have any unfunded retirement liabilities?

(7) What is the city's budget schedule for the upcoming year? When will the public be able to participate in the budget process?

You should now have some basic skills to help you get involved in some fascinating city budget discussions.

At a time in our nation's history, when confidence in elected officials at every level of government is at an all time low, knowledgeable citizens are needed more than ever to help ensure good governance.

Welcome to the government envisioned by Thomas Jefferson more than 200 years ago. Let's make him proud. Enjoy your newly acquired government budgeting skills and get out there and help shape the decisions that impact your community.

Though (the people) may acquiesce, they cannot approve what they do not understand.

Thomas Jefferson, 1792 Opinion on Apportionment Bill, ME 3:211

CLASS ASSIGNMENTS

Here are some class assignments to use if you are using this book as part of a class or workshop on city budgets. They can be done either in a small group or individually.

Identify a city and find their budget document online. I encourage my students to select a city with which they have some familiarity. Some city budget documents do not present their budget with good summaries making it difficult to find some of the key information. It is, therefore, helpful to see some examples of good budget documents designed to inform citizens. The Government Finance Officers Association conducts a Distinguished Budget Presentation Awards program and the lists of the winners along with links to those budgets documents are on their website at www. gfoa.org.

I would recommend using one or more of these award winning budget documents to see examples of good summary information.

Paper Assignment: Use this book to help you write an analysis of the city's current budget document. Your paper will include the following sections:

- A brief description of the city, including basic demographics, location, and the services provided by the city, the total budget amount, and the total of the general fund budget.

- Discuss the major revenue sources in the city's general fund and how and why they have changed for the coming budget year.

- Discuss any changes being made to city services and why they have to be changed for the coming year. Include what changes are being made to the city's workforce, i.e., new hires, layoffs, furloughs, increases or concessions in salaries and benefits, etc.

- Discuss any long term financial issues facing the city and what the city may have to do in the future, i.e., unfunded liabilities, falling real estate prices, termination of a temporary sales tax, etc. that will reduce city revenue and require services to be reduced.

- Discuss your overall impression of the city's budget document. Does it explain what is happening to the city's revenue and expenditures? Is the information clear? Include a list of at least three recommendations on how the budget document could be improved, i.e., what information was missing or difficult to find, or what type of charts would help citizens better understand the city's budget.

- Include the following attachments to your paper. For some cities you may have to create your own pie charts based on information in the budget document. Be sure your pie chart title includes the total dollar amount of what you are showing, the time period represented by the chart. Label each category of the pie chart with the name of the category and the percentage. Show individual categories with 10% or more of the total and group the smaller categories together as "Other".
  - o Pie chart showing the general fund and other funds that make up the total city budget
  - o Pie chart showing the revenue sources in the general fund
  - o Pie chart showing the department expenditures in the general fund
  - o Table showing the number of positions or full time equivalents (FTEs) by department

Presentation Assignment: Use your paper to develop a 10-15 minute presentation explaining the city's budget. Acting as the city's finance staff make a presentation (with PowerPoint slides) describing the city's budget at a public meeting to describe the current year's budget after adoption by the city council. The purpose of the presentation is to inform citizens of the city about the budget for the coming year. For tables and graphs, show individual categories with 10% or more of the total and group the smaller categories together as "Other".

The presentation will include the following:

- The total amount of the budget the city council adopted.
- The total amount of the general fund budget.
- General fund revenues
  - o Pie chart showing the revenue sources for the general fund
  - o Bar graph showing trends in the major revenue sources for the past 3-5 years.
  - o A list of major revenue issues facing the city.
- General fund expenditures
  - o Pie chart showing the spending on the major departments for the general fund.
  - o Table showing the five largest departments' total budget for past three years.
  - o A list of major expenditure issues facing the city.
- Table showing total number of positions (FTEs) in each department for past three years.
- Conclusion: – Summarize major budget issues facing the city. Include the city council's budget schedule this past year including when they adopted the budget..

ABOUT THE AUTHOR

Mary Jo Zenk has been analyzing government budgets for over 25 years. She has been involved in all aspects of government budgeting from preparation, discussions, deliberations and adoption, to implementation and monitoring. Ms. Zenk has held executive positions in several public agencies with responsibilities central to financial management and operations. She has analyzed the financial situation of agencies, developed operating and capital budgets, and currently teaches budgeting and public financial management at California State University Monterey Bay.

Ms Zenk now runs her own management consulting business providing technical assistance to government agencies and nonprofits. She excels at helping local elected officials and nonprofit board members learn enough about financial management and budgeting to provide appropriate financial oversight.

She has an uncanny ability to take a government budget document, the size of a phone book, and reduce it to a four page newsletter, often called a 'Budget-in-Brief'.

Ms. Zenk has a B.S. in Business from Santa Clara University, a Master of Public Management from the University of Maryland and is a Certified Public Accountant.

More information about the services Ms. Zenk provides can be found at www.zenkconsulting.com or by contacting her at info@zenkconsulting.com

GLOSSARY

Here are some terms you may find in the budget
document or mentioned during council meetings.[9]

Account – A separate financial reporting unit for budgeting,
management, or accounting purposes. Every transaction, starting with
the adoption of the budget is recorded in an account.

Accrual basis – A method of accounting in which revenues are
recorded when measurable and earned, and expenses are recognized
when a good or service is used.

---

[9] This glossary is a composite of others including the glossaries in *Management Policies
in Local Government Finance, 5th edition,* edited by A. Richard Aronson and Eli Schwart,
published by the International City/County Management Association (ICMA), 2004
and *Budgeting: A Budgetary Guide for Local Government, 2nd edition,* by Robert L. Bland,
published by ICMA Press, 2007.

Activity – A departmental effort that contributes to the accomplishment of specific program objectives.

Allotment - The distribution of budget authority by an agency to various subunits or regional offices.

Appropriation - Legal authorization to make expenditures or enter into obligations for specific purposes.

Assessed property value – The value assigned to property for the purpose of levying property taxes.

Asset account – A type of account that records information on things of value to a fund. Asset accounts are of two general types: current assets, such as cash or things that can quickly be converted into cash, and fixed assets, or things of value with a life expectancy of more than one year, such as land.

Balance sheet – One of the basic financial statements prepared by local government for each fund or fund group that reports asset, liabilities and fund balances. The "balance" occurs because, at any point in time, a fund's total assets will always equal the sum of its liabilities and fund balance.

Balanced budget – A budget in which current revenues equal current expenditures. After expenditures have been reduced, budgets may be balanced by adjusting taxes and fees to generate total current revenues, by drawing down fund balances accumulated from prior years, or by short term borrowings to make up the difference between revenues from taxes and other income and current expenditures. The legal requirements for a balanced budget may be set by state or the local government.

Balanced scorecard – An approach to budgeting that uses a local government's mission and strategic plan to develop ten to fifteen key measures of success by which the city or county will judge its overall performance. One key measure of success is citizen satisfaction with a local government's performance. Budget decisions are made on the basis of strategic priorities, and a scorecard is kept on how effectively performance improves in the key performance areas.

Base budget – A budget that provides an estimate of the spending authority needed to continue current levels of services with no changes in the level of effort. A base budget provides a benchmark for evaluating the effect of any proposed spending or revenue changes on the budget. It nets out one-time expenditures or other special appropriations to provide managers with an accurate estimate of the true cost of continuing operations at the existing level of effort.

Benchmark – A standard of expected performance that is used as a measurement to compare against actual performance. Benchmarks can be established internally on the basis of historical trends or externally from sources such as "best practices" or from other local governments. They may also be formulated by independent professional associations or by federal and state agencies.

Biennial budget – A budget that covers a two-year period.

Bond – A promise to repay borrowed money on a particular date, often ten or twenty years in the future; most bonds involve a promise to pay a specified dollar amount of interest at predetermined intervals.

Budget amendment – A revision of the adopted budget that, when approved by the council, replaces the original provision. Budget amendments occur frequently throughout the fiscal year, as spending priorities shift.

Bond anticipation note (BAN) – See short term debt.

Budget - A spending plan that balances revenues and expenditures over a fixed time period (usually a year) and that includes, at least by implication, a work plan.

Budget authority – Authority provided through an appropriation act approved by the council to enter into financial commitments, such as contracts and purchase orders that will result in the eventual disbursement of cash. In the case of the operating budget, most budget authority lapses at the end of the fiscal year if the authority has not been committed at that point. In the case of the capital budget, authority may not lapse until construction of the project is completed.

Budget calendar – A timetable showing when particular tasks must be completed in order for the governing body to approve the spending plan before the beginning of the next fiscal year.

Budget cycle – The recurring process, either annual or biennial, in which a government prepares, adopts and implements a spending plan.

Budget deficit – The result of current expenditures exceeding current revenues. The difference must be covered through either borrowing or using budget reserves.

Budget guidelines – Guidelines developed by the chief executive in consultation with the council that describe the budget environment – that is revenue expectations and policy emphases – for the forthcoming year. Departments make their budget requests based on the guidelines.

Budget manual – A booklet prepared by the budget or finance office that includes at a minimum, the budget calendar, the forms that departments need to prepare their requests, and a description of the budget process.

Budget reserve – Money accumulated in special accounts for future purposes, for example, to deal with unforeseen circumstances or to replace buildings or equipment. Some cities have more than one reserve with one for major emergencies, such as a natural disaster.

Budget transfer – The shifting of budget authority from one account or fund to another after the council has adopted the budget. Authority to make such transfers is granted either explicitly in charter or law, or implicitly by agreement between the council and the manager.

Budgeting for outcomes – An entrepreneurial approach to budget preparation that relies on competition among departments and programs to promote innovative solutions to community problems.

Capital asset – An item that costs a considerable amount of money and is intended to last a long time, such as a building. Also referred to as a fixed asset.

Capital budget – A spending plan for the acquisition or improvements to land, facilities or infrastructure. The capital budget (1) balances revenues and expenditures, (2) specifies the sources of revenues, (3) lists each project or acquisition, and (4) must ordinarily be approved by a legislative body.

Capital improvements program (CIP) – A plan that identifies the capital projects to be funded during the planning horizon (usually five years). The CIP may list anticipated revenues to pay for the projects. The CIP is usually updated annually, and the first year of the plan may serve as the current-year capital budget.

Capital outlay – Spending on fixed assets; generally, such expenditures exceed a specified amount or are for purchases intended to last more than one year.

Capital projects fund – Governmental funds established to account for the acquisition of large capital improvements other than those accounted for in enterprise or fiduciary funds.

Cash basis – A method of accounting in which revenues are recorded only when cash is received and expenditures are recorded only when payment is made.

Cash flow – The net cash balance at any given point. The treasurer prepares a cash budget that projects the inflow, outflow, and net balance of cash reserves on a daily, weekly, and monthly basis.

Chart of accounts – A chart that assigns a unique number to each type of account (e.g. salaries or property taxes) and to each budgetary unit in the organization. The chart of accounts provides a system for recording revenues and expenditures that fits the organizational structure.

Collective bargaining – The process of negotiation between representatives of workers, usually labor union officials, and management to determine the conditions of employment. The agreement reached may cover not only wages but hiring practices, layoffs, promotions, working conditions and hours, and benefit programs.

Comprehensive annual financial report (CAFR) – Usually referred to by its abbreviation, this report summarizes financial data for the previous fiscal year in a standardized format and includes an auditor's report.

Contingency account – An account set aside to meet unforeseen circumstances.

Cost effective measures – Performance measures that are the ratio of inputs to outcomes and that gauge the changes, if any, that occur in a program objective (outcome) as a result of changes in its funding (inputs).

Cost of Living Allowance or COLA - This is the automatic annual rate increase for salaries. It is usually negotiated in collective bargaining agreements.

Council resolution – A formal agreement directing certain actions take place for the city. This formal agreement must be approved by a majority vote of the city council.

Credit – An accounting term used in bookkeeping to indicate the right column of entry, as opposed to the left (or debit) column, for entering a transaction. A credit entry increases the balance in a liability account but decreases the balance in an asset account.

Debt policy – A policy that established the guidelines for an issuer's use of debt.

Debit – An accounting term used in double-entry bookkeeping to indicate the left column of entry, as opposed to the right (or credit) column, for entering a transaction. A debit entry increases the balance in an asset account but decreases the balance in a liability account.

Debt service – Annual principal and interest payments that the local government owes on money it has borrowed.

Debt service fund – A fund established to account for revenues and expenditures used to repay the principal and interest on debt.

Decision package – A term originally used with zero-based budgeting to describe the various levels of spending proposals that departments use in submitting their budget requests.

Default – Failure to make a debt payment (principal or interest) on time.

Depreciation – A type of expense associated with the use of fixed assets other than land. The annual depreciation of fixed assets is reported on the financial statements of funds using the accrual basis of accounting.

Direct costs – Expenses that are directly attributable to the production of a service, such as wages, benefits, supplies, contract services, and that would be eliminated if the service was discontinued.

Disbursement – Payment for goods or services that have been delivered and invoiced.

Earmarking – Legal limitations on the revenue from fees, licenses, taxes or grants that determines how the funds may be spent.

Economies of scale – The cost savings that usually occur with increases in output. If the number of units increases, fixed costs are divided among the units.

Encumbrance – Budget authority that is set aside when a purchase order or contract is approved. It assures suppliers that sufficient funds will be available once the order if filled. Also known as an obligation.

Enterprise fund – A separate fund used to account for services – for example, water, sewer, golf and airports – that are supported primarily by service charges paid by users.

Entitlement program – A program in which funding is allocated according to eligibility criteria; any agency or citizen that meets the criteria specified in the law receives the benefit.

Entrepreneurial budgeting – Budget preparation procedures that interject market like measures, such as competition and performance contracting into budget deliberations. Such procedures include budgeting for outcomes, balanced scorecard, and responsibility-center management.

Expenditures – An accounting term that refers to a payment or disbursement. The expenditure may be for the purchase of an asset, a reduction of a liability, a distribution to the owners, or could be an expense.

Expense – An accounting term that refers to a cost that has expired, used up, or was necessary in order to earn the revenues during the time period indicated in the heading of the income statement.

Fiduciary fund – A fund that accounts for resources that a government holds in trust for individuals or other governments.

Financial report – A formal record of the financial activities of the organization.

Fiscal Year – A designated twelve-month period for budgeting and record-keeping purposes.

Fixed asset – See capital asset

Full-time equivalent (FTE) – The number of hours per year that a full time employee is expected to work during the year. For part time employees, FTEs are computed as the fraction of hours worked to the total number of hours worked in the work year (usually 2,080 hours).

Fund – A self-balancing set of accounts. Government accounting information is organized into funds, each with separate revenues, expenditures or expenses and fund balances.

Fund accounting - A general term used to describe the use of funds in recording, reconciling, and reporting financial transactions.

Fund balance – The difference between a fund's assets and its liabilities. Portions of the fund balance may be reserved for various purposes and for emergencies.

Furlough -Temporary unpaid days off usually spread out over the year or during a slow period. For example, the city may furlough staff one day per week and close its offices to the public every Friday to save money.

General fund – The major fund in most government units; accounts for all activities, especially tax-funded functions, such as police and fire protection, not accounted for in other funds.

Generally accepted accounting principles (GAAP) – Uniform minimum standards used by state and local governments for financial recording and reporting; established by the accounting profession through the Governmental Accounting Standards Board.

General obligation bonds (GO) – A bond that is backed by the government's unconditional ability to raise taxes.

Governmental Accounting Standards Board (GASB) – The professional account body that sets accounting standards for governmental entities at the state and local levels.

Grant – A payment of money, often earmarked for a specific purpose or program, from one governmental unit to another or from a governmental unit to a not-for-profit agency.

Incremental budgeting – A budgeting process in which the preceding year determines how funds will be allocated among departments and programs; increases in allocation usually occur in small increments over past levels.

Indirect cost – Costs that are incidental to the production of goods and services, such as administration, budgeting, accounting, personnel, purchasing, legal, and similar staff support services. Unlike direct costs, indirect costs do not disappear if the service or good is discontinued. Also known as overhead.

Infrastructure – Basic public investments, such as roads, storm drainage, water and sewer lines, streetlights and sidewalks.

Interfund activity or transfer – The transfer of money from one fund to another in a governmental unit; such transfers usually require the approval of the governing body and are subject to restrictions in state and local law.

Interim financial reports – Quarterly or monthly comparisons of budgeted with actual revenues and expenditures to date. These reports provide decision makers with an early warning of impending expenditure overruns or revenue shortfalls.

Internal service fund – A fund that accounts for the goods and services provided by one department (i.e., information technology or fleet management) to another on a fee-for-service basis.

Lapse in budget authority – A provision usually contained in an appropriation act that any unused budget authority lapses at the end of the fiscal year (or biennium for governments on a two year cycle). Any unspent or unencumbered balances remaining at the end of the year lapse into the fund balance.

Liability account – A type of account that contains information on claims in the fund's assets, either by other funds of the local government or by external entities.

Line-item budget – A budget format in which departmental outlays are grouped according to the items that will be purchased, with one item or group of items on each line.

Mandate – A requirement from a higher level of government that a lower level of government perform a task, usually to meet a particular standard, and often without compensation. This is often an unfunded mandate from the higher level of government.

Merit system – The process of promoting and hiring government employees based on their ability to perform a job, rather than on their political connections.

Modified accrual basis – A form of accrual accounting in which (1) expenditures are recognized when the goods or services are received and (2) revenues, such as taxes, are recognized when measurable and available to pay expenditures in the current accounting period.

Net assets – Under the accrual basis of accounting for governments, the difference between assets and liabilities.

Objects of expenditure – Items to be purchased in an operating budget such as personnel or operating.

Operating budget – The portion of a budget that deals with recurring expenditures such as salaries, electric bills, postage, printing and duplication, paper supplies, and gasoline.

Operating deficit - The amount by which this year's, or this budget period's, revenues are exceeded by expenditures for the same period; does not take into account any balances left over from prior years.

Operating statement – See statement of revenues, expenditures and changes in fund balance.

Outcomes – Measures of the amount of work accomplished, such as the number of citizens served, the number of hours expended, or the number of emergency calls processed.

Overhead – See indirect cost.

Parcel tax – A parcel tax is a flat amount (e.g. $100 per property) which is charged on each parcel of property for a specific government service and usually for a limited time period.

Pay-as-you-go financing – Also referred to as "pay-go". A method for paying for capital projects that relies on current tax, reserves and grant revenues rather than on debt.

Pay-as- you-use financing – The use of debt rather than current revenues to pay for capital outlays.

Payback period – For income producing ventures, such as a utility infrastructure improvements, the length of time required to recover the cost of an investment.

Pay grade – A system of monetary compensation for employment, commonly used in public service. Pay grades encompass two dimensions: a "vertical" range where each level corresponds to the responsibility of, and requirements needed for a certain position; and a "horizontal" range within this scale sometimes known as steps to allow for monetary incentives rewarding the employee's quality of performance or length of service.

Payments in lieu of taxes (PILOT or PILTS) – Compensation from tax-exempt institutes in return for local government services.

Pension trust fund – A type of fiduciary fund that governments hold in trust on behalf of their employees or the employees of other governments.

Performance budgeting – A budget format that includes (1) performance goals and objectives and (2) demand, workload, efficiency, and effectiveness (outcome or impact) measures for each governmental program.

Performance measures – Calculations used in budgets to show, for example, (1) the amount of work accomplished, (2) the efficiency with which tasks were completed, and (3) the effectiveness of a program, which is often expressed as the extent to which objectives were met.

Performance based budgeting – The entire planning and budgeting framework is results oriented and is a way to allocate resources for achieving certain results.

Program - A set of activities with a common goal.

Program budgeting – A budget format that organizes budgeting information and allocates funds along program rather than department lines. A program is a set of activities with a common goal.

Property tax rate – A rate of taxation set either by a local governing board or in state law, that, when applied to the tax base (assessed value), represents the property owner's tax liability. If not set by state, the rate is typically set by the local government as part of deliberations on the operating budget and is adjusted to bring current revenues into balance with current expenditures.

Proprietary fund – A class of fund types that account for a local government's businesslike activities. Proprietary funds are of two types: enterprise funds and internal service funds. Both use accrual basis of accounting and receive revenues from charges to users.

Public hearing – An open meeting regarding proposed operating or capital budget allocations that provide citizens with an opportunity to voice their view on the merits of the proposals.

Purchase order (PO) – An agreement to buy goods and services from a specific vendor, with a promise to pay on delivery.

Purchase requisition – A formal application which, when completed by the department, initiates the purchase process. Once approved and issued to the vendor, the purchase requisition becomes a purchase order.

Rainy day fund – Revenue stabilization reserve that provides resources when tax revenues temporarily decline as the result of a recession, the loss of a major taxpayer, or other similar circumstances.

Reserves – Money accumulated for future purposes.

Revenue bond – A bond backed by revenues from the project that the borrowed money was used to create, expand, or improve.

Revenue stabilization reserve – See rainy day fund.

Salary savings – The reduced expenditures for salaries that result when a position remains unfilled for part of a year or when a more senior employee is replaced by a newer employee at a lower salary. Also known as salary lapse.

Short term debt – A type of debt issued when a local government encounters a cash flow deficit or wishes to begin a major capital project before bonds are sold. Short-term debt may be issued as tax anticipation notes (TANs) or bond anticipation notes (BANs) to meet short term cash needs. The anticipated tax or bond revenue provides the collateral for repayment.

Special revenue fund – A fund used to account for revenues legally earmarked for a particular purpose. For example, if revenues from a hotel/motel occupancy tax are earmarked for tourism and convention development, a separate hotel/motel tax fund would fund would be established for the revenue and expenditures associated with that purpose.

Statement of revenues, expenditures, and changes in fund balance For governmental funds, a financial statement that compares revenues with expenditures for the reporting period and reflects the increase or decrease in fund balance that occurs. Also known as an operating statement.

Step increase – See pay grade.

Strategic plan – A type of plan that provides for the goals, objectives, and strategies for a local government or one of its units.

Target-based budgeting (TBB) – A budgeting process in which departments are provided with a maximum level for their budget requests. The budget office requires separate justification for proposed spending levels that exceed that target.

Tax anticipation note (TAN) – See short term debt

Tax expenditures – Partial or full exemptions, tax credits, deductions, from taxes or other forgone tax revenues.

Tax expenditure limitation (TEL) – A state or local law that provides relief to taxpayers by restricting either a local government's taxing powers or its spending discretion.

Trust fund – A fund established to receive money that the local government holds on behalf of individuals or other governments.

Unfunded liability – A liability that accrues to a fund for which there is no source of revenue. In recent years, the Government Accounting Standards Board, through its pronouncements, has sought to hold local and state governments more accountable for fully disclosing the long-term cost of unfunded liabilities such as health benefits for future retirees. If funds for this future obligation are not set aside while the employees are working, it shifts the cost of the prior year commitments to future taxpayers.

Unfunded mandate – See mandate

Unreserved fund balance – Money left over from prior years that is not committed for other purposes and that can be allocated in the upcoming budget.

Zero-base budgeting – A budget process under which (1) departments prepare decision packages representing various service levels and rank them; (2) departmental rankings are merged across the whole governmental unit to form a single, ranked list; and (3) funding is allocated to each successive item in the list until the money runs out.

.

ADDITIONAL RESOURCES

The following national organizations are good resources for local government budget and financial information:

Government Finance Officers Association (GFOA)
http://www.gfoa.org

International City/County Management Association (ICMA)
http://icma.org

National League of Cities
http://www.nlc.org

In addition, there are regional and state-wide associations affiliated with these organizations.

CPSIA information can be obtained at www.ICGtesting.com
Printed in the USA
LVOW07s0007280815

451797LV00033B/1547/P